PrayerStarters

In Times of
Pain or Illness

GW00384699

Text © 1999 by Alaric Lewis, O.S.B.
Published by One Caring Place
Abbey Press
St. Meinrad, Indiana 47577

All rights reserved.
No part of this book may be used or reproduced
in any manner without written permission of the
publisher, except in the case of brief quotations
embodied in critical articles and reviews.

Library of Congress Catalog Number
99-72387

ISBN 0-87029-327-3

Printed in the United States of America

PrayerStarters

In Times of
Pain or Illness

by Alaric Lewis, O.S.B.

ONE
CARING
PLACE

Abbey Press

Introduction

In 1995, I was informed by my doctor that what I had assumed to be a harmless tumor was instead cancer. In the hours that followed the news, I experienced a multitude of emotions: fear, sadness, anger, frustration, despair. My mind was filled with plans, probabilities, and possibilities; I felt completely overwhelmed to cope with it all.

Life had been good before my diagnosis. I was a priest serving in a wonderful, active parish and was overjoyed to be doing the kinds of things that I was doing: preaching, teaching, comforting the sick and those who mourned, helping people to pray. With the words "You have cancer" came an enormous change within and around me, and so many of the things that

I had once enjoyed began to be cast in a different light. How could I preach about the love of God when that love seemed less real to me?

How could I teach about the wonders of faith when my own faith seemed fragile, tenuous? What words of comfort could I offer the sick and mourning, when the very words I used to share with these people seemed empty, meaningless? How could I help others to pray when I found prayer so difficult myself, wondering if my words were even heard at all?

It became obvious to me that prayer—communication with God—had not ceased, nor had God's love for me. It was simply that the confusing circumstances of my life had so changed my outlook that I wasn't quite sure what to do anymore. The desire to pray was there; but prayer itself was difficult.

Such struggles are quite common, and this book is written to help people who may be experiencing just such confusion in their lives. It offers reflections, exercises, and guides to help move people in the direction of prayer, to inspire words and actions when those words and actions are difficult to find. It seeks to help the reader know that even in a life that can be filled with confusion and sadness, God is somehow in the midst of it all, desperate to listen to us, to speak to us. Ultimately, this book is written not so much to help the reader begin prayer, but rather to continue that divine communication which already exists, and will exist until the end of time.

It's Not Always Easy

*"In the difficult are the friendly forces,
the hands that work on us."*
—Rainer Maria Rilke

Prayer is not always easy. If our prayer consists of words, sometimes it is difficult to say anything. If our prayer consists of listening, sometimes it is difficult to hear anything. If our prayer consists of activities, sometimes it is difficult to find the energy and the focus to do anything.

In the difficulties of life, however, there also can we find strength. If words and insights and actions seem just beyond our reach at times, that's fine. We can rest assured that God's hand is at work even in our difficulties, and recognition of this fact is a prayer in itself.

PrayerStarters

Take a moment to reflect on what may be causing difficulty in your prayer life. In a quiet, safe place, say these things out loud. Saying them won't make the difficulties go away, but when these things are outside of us, they hold us less in their power.

Dear God,

Because of these obstacles, I am finding it difficult to pray. I understand that these difficulties may not end, but help me to know that you are near me, even when my words and actions can't seem to communicate that.

Giving Pain Its Due

"An hour of pain is as long as a day of pleasure."
—English proverb

People deal with physical pain in a variety of ways: ignoring it, lamenting it, cursing it, sedating it. Whatever our method, the fact remains that physical pain takes a great deal of our energy. When we are hurting, we simply cannot do some of the things that we once did.

Pain, however, is also our body's way of telling us that something is wrong; it is a mode of communication to us, and to God. So we must not ignore it completely, as even the harshest of communications can still have meaning for us if we strive to have open minds and hearts.

PrayerStarters

Sit in a comfortable position and breathe slowly and deeply, concentrating on the physical sensations that are present in your body.

Imagine that these sensations are voices, expressing what needs God's touch within you.

Dear God,
My body is telling me _____. With each breath, help me to feel your soothing presence. Give me the strength to bear my pain, and don't let it cause me to close my mind or heart to what you may be telling me.

Getting Real

"Listen to me, O God, as I complain."
—Psalm 63

Sometimes we have a tendency to "sanitize" our prayer, limiting it to respectful petitions or pious platitudes. The People of Israel knew that virtually any emotion was a springboard for prayer, as evidenced by the passionate prayers in the Book of Psalms.

Anger—even anger directed at God—is a natural by-product of being sick. Questions sometimes asked in anger—"Why is this happening to me?" "What did I ever do to deserve this?" "Why does my poor family have to go through all this too?"—are questions that we should not be afraid to ask. God understands our anger, and can take it. Indeed God can allow our anger to become prayer.

PrayerStarters

Make an anger list. What situations or people make you angry?

_____ _____ _____

_____ _____ _____

_____ _____ _____

Dear God,

There are times when I am angry, even angry at you. Help me to know that my anger is natural, and in acknowledging and voicing it, help me to begin to let go of it.

Pain—and Hope—in Common

"Although the world is full of suffering,
it is full also of the overcoming of it."
—Helen Keller

All we need to do to be aware of the universality of suffering is to watch the evening news. There are always reports of ordinary people all over the world struggling through suffering, due to natural disasters, war, famine, injustice. Suffering is a part of the human condition, and will always be among us.

Although God allows suffering to happen, and can even teach important lessons from it, God does not impose suffering on people to "pay them back" for anything they might have done in their life. If we are sick, it is because we are a part of the human race, and sickness and suffering are part of being human.

PrayerStarters

Pick up a newspaper or watch a news broadcast. Pay close attention to the reports of suffering that you hear. See in these stories not faceless individuals, but brothers and sisters who share the commonality of suffering with you. Know that as you struggle, so they struggle.

Dear God,
Please hear my prayers on behalf of _____, and all people who suffer this day. As their lives have been filled with the reality of that part of the human condition, so too may they be filled with other realities of that same condition—the wonder of life, the beauty of nature, the kindness of people.

Light in the Darkness

"Hearts live by being wounded."
—Oscar Wilde, *A Woman of No Importance*

One of the most perplexing mysteries of Christianity is that of the redemptive value of suffering. How can it be that suffering can bring about growth? How can it be that being wounded can somehow bring about healing? How can it be that dying can somehow bring about new life?

Even though a realization of some value in suffering doesn't ease the burden of the suffering itself, it can be the only beacon of light in the dark confusion that can accompany sickness and suffering. We can trust in God's confusing, mysterious providence and know that somehow the very depths of our distress can bring us insight and grace.

PrayerStarters

Reflect on the image of a seed buried in the ground. Surrounded by the seeming cold indifference of the earth, the seed begins to change, its shell traumatically cracked open. But from this distress comes the first inklings of new life. And eventually a plant, filled with beauty and promise, emerges, triumphant over the darkness, triumphant over the pain.

Dear God,

Help me to bear the situations in my life that cause me to suffer, and may they somehow strengthen me with wisdom and insight into the mystery of your love. Help me to see your hand at work, even in suffering.

Deo Gratias

"Bees sip honey from flowers
and hum their thanks when they leave."
—Rabindranath Tagore, *Stray Birds*

Gracias ... Merci ... Danke ... Tak ... In any language, some of the most beautiful words are those words which express gratitude. The human spirit is at its best when recognizing the blessings that are all around.

When our minds and hearts are influenced by sickness, it is all too easy to forget the good things that continue to surround us. Recognizing all the things for which we can be grateful is a vital tool in keeping our lives balanced, in not letting the sickness take too large a possession of our very souls.

PrayerStarters

Make a gratitude list. For what situations or people are you most thankful?

_____ _____ _____

_____ _____ _____

_____ _____ _____

Dear God,

Help me to be ever mindful of the blessings with which you have surrounded me in this world. Never let the darkness of sickness obscure the light of gracious gifts I have been given. Help me to be a grateful person.

Inching Closer to God

"Many strokes overthrow the tallest oaks."
—John Lyly, Euphues: The Anatomy of Wit

Perseverance is a testimony to the strength of the human spirit; it is that strength which is present whenever any person, keeping at something, is able to scale "insurmountable" heights.

Prayer requires just such a spirit of perseverance, most especially when we also face the challenges of sickness. When it seems that our plate is full, that we couldn't possibly sit down and pray, we need to recognize that if we move forward in prayer—bit by bit, taking small steps—we can inch closer to the God who waits for us.

PrayerStarters

Make a list of prayerful words/actions/gestures/ideas that were expressed today, even if it is only one thought or a simple action that could be described as "prayerful." Make a resolution to match that list tomorrow and, if possible, add to it by one. Keep the list expanding bit by bit.

Dear God,
Sometimes I want to give up—on people, on you, on situations. Help me to stick with it, to tap into that within me which allows me to keep going, even when I feel like quitting. Help me to know that you are with me with each small step I take.

What Will Happen?

"Grief has limits, whereas apprehension has none.
For we grieve only what we know has happened,
but we fear all that possibly may happen."
—Pliny the Younger

"Don't worry; everything will be fine," words that are often spoken in an effort to temper anxiety, all too often may fall on deaf ears. Anxiety about what may happen to us can so grip us that this worry begins to affect us in ways that it shouldn't, obscuring our vision of life.

Although anxiety is a reality of the human condition, peace is a reality of the divine condition. In the midst of unknowns, God offers us an image of one so in love with creation that even the needs of the sparrows themselves are tended to.

PrayerStarters

Make a list of the "unknowns" in your life, things that cause you concern and worry.

_____   _____   _____

_____   _____   _____

_____   _____   _____

Go through the list slowly, and ask God to relieve each worry. Imagine as you speak each worry aloud that God is taking on this worry, and replacing it with peace and love.

God Alongside

"Turn my mind to you when I am lonely."
—Psalm 24

People often equate loneliness with being alone, but people can feel lonely even in the largest of crowds. A perfect example of this is when we are patients in the hospital: being surrounded by doctors, nurses, and visitors cannot always take away the feeling that we're alone, that no one quite understands what it is we're feeling.

No one but God, of course. Like a mother gently wiping the fevered brow of her child, God is constantly present to us, eternally "checking in on us" so that we need not feel alone. Trust that presence, and allow it to strengthen your weakness.

PrayerStarters

Reflect on a time in your life when you felt surrounded by love. Imagine the feelings associated with that time, and recognize that God was present. Realize that God is just as present right now, at this moment.

Dear God,
Even when I feel all alone, help me to realize that you are with me. When I am uncertain, be my surety; when I am weary, be my strength; when I am filled with sorrow, be my joy; when I am confused, be my clarity; and when I am lonely, be my companion.

The Healing Power of Laughter

*"The most wasted day is that in which
we have not laughed."*
—Chamfort, *Maximes et pensées*

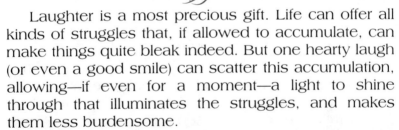

Laughter is a most precious gift. Life can offer all kinds of struggles that, if allowed to accumulate, can make things quite bleak indeed. But one hearty laugh (or even a good smile) can scatter this accumulation, allowing—if even for a moment—a light to shine through that illuminates the struggles, and makes them less burdensome.

Some would say that in the face of sickness laughter might be inappropriate. Nonsense! In the face of sickness, laughter can be just the medicine needed.

PrayerStarters

Reflect on a joke, story, or incident that made you laugh at the time; call your funniest friend; watch a funny movie. Allow the refreshment of humor to invigorate your soul once again. Laugh again, if you can; and if you can't, smile.

Dear God;

Thank you for all those times in my life when humor has lifted my spirits. Especially in my times of need, help me to continue to experience the rich gift of laughter that is your most precious gift.

The Gift of Tears

"To weep is to make less the depth of grief."
—William Shakespeare, *Henry VI*

———— ✦ ————

The Desert Fathers and Mothers, those early Christian men and women who went out to the desert to immerse themselves in prayer, often used to pray for the gift of tears. Tears can be beautiful punctuation marks in the wondrous poetry that is life; they help give meaning and inflection to a variety of emotions.

We should not be afraid to cry, afraid to receive such a gift. Keeping a stiff upper lip will ultimately do little more than make our lips tired, whereas a good cry can cleanse and refresh us.

PrayerStarters

Reflect on the last time you wept. After the tears had stopped, what were your feelings? Is there anything in your life now that could benefit from that same feeling, from those same tears?

Dear God,
    As Jesus wept, so too may I know the power of tears. Please send me the gift of tears, that I may be refreshed by their presence. If they are of sadness, may the tears fill up the well of grief; if they are of joy, may the tears be as drops in a sea of happiness.

Helping Hands

*"Sir, I have no one to put me into the pool
when the water is stirred up."*

—John 5: 7

Many of us are fiercely independent people. We don't like to have to ask for anyone's help; we prefer to do things for ourselves. Having to ask someone for help is an act of vulnerability, and no one likes feeling vulnerable.

The fact of the matter is, however, that we do need the help of others at various times in our lives. And if we don't allow others to help us, it can be as if we are like the man in John's gospel, unable to reach the refreshing waters of the pool. Let us not block ourselves from the compassion-drenched refreshment of the help of others.

PrayerStarters

Make a list of things that you really need right now in your life.

_____   _____   _____

_____   _____   _____

Now make a list of people who could help you in fulfilling these needs.

_____   _____   _____

_____   _____   _____

Dear God,
    Help me to accept the help of others.

Doctoring Your Spirit

"Are any among you sick? They should call for the elders of the church and have them pray over them, anointing them with oil in the name of the Lord."
—The Letter of James 5:14

Throughout the ages people have been called forth to tend to the spiritual needs of their communities, to help others open their eyes, ears, and hearts to the wonder of divinity that swirls around and throughout the earth.

Finding a "doctor of souls" during a time of illness is equally as important as finding a doctor of medicine. Those involved in spiritual care are not necessarily holier or closer to God than anyone else, but they do have training and experience to help others realize the particular closeness to God.

PrayerStarters

Consider making an appointment with a priest, rabbi, minister, or any spiritual guide.

Are there areas you could discuss with him or her in which you want to feel closer to God?

Can you ask him or her to help you in these areas?

Dear God,

I know that your loving kindness surrounds me, even if I sometimes find it difficult to see, to feel. Please send people into my life who will help turn my spirit closer to you, and so bring me to wholeness, to love.

The Nearness Is All

"Friendship multiplies the good of life and divides the evil.
'Tis the sole remedy against misfortune,
the very ventilation of the soul."
—Baltasar Gracián, *The Art of Worldly Wisdom*

There is great comfort in a good friend. Friends can help cheer us in our sorrows, strengthen us in our weakness, give clarity to our confusion, and offer love when we feel alone. While the world can offer us the transitory, a true friend can offer us permanence.

Just as we know that our friends can count on us when they need us, we also need to know that we can count on them when we need them. Asking for help, finding a shoulder to cry on, sharing a laugh—what friend would not want to offer such expressions? What friend would not want to help us multiply the good of life?

PrayerStarters

Write a letter to a friend.

Dear _____,

Thank you for your presence in my life. I count your friendship among my greatest treasures.

Knowing that you will help with whatever I need, I would like _____. It would be my joy to some day help you out as well.

Dear God,

Thank you so much for my friends; they help me know that you are near.

United in Prayer

"For where two or three are gathered in my name, I am there among them."
—Matthew 18:20

There is strength in numbers. Witness the frenetic activity of a beehive. Individually, each bee contributes but a tiny fraction of what is needed for the common goal. But together, working, swarming, humming the sweet melodies of their commonality, golden luscious honey is produced.

We are not unlike these bees. And whereas individual prayer is a vital part of life, prayer together with our brothers and sisters helps make us aware of how connected we all are. There is strength and beauty in praying together, as our common voices combine in the sweet melody of all things possible in God.

PrayerStarters

Make a point to pray with others sometime this week—either in church or in a smaller, less formal setting.

Imagine that the common strength of those around you praying is strengthening your own body and soul as well.

Imagine that your needs and concerns—even if voiced in the quiet of your heart—are being expressed by everyone present.

The Power of the Word

"Thank God for books!"
—Henry Ward Beecher, *Proverbs from Plymouth Pulpit*

Whether it is a child discovering Doctor Seuss for the first time, or one getting lost in Shakespeare, or even the guilty pleasure of a romance novel—reading has the ability to open to us worlds that can shed light and insight on the world in which we live.

Literature has the ability to temper our moods. When it is good to be sad, it can share our sadness. If we need to move away from sadness, it can introduce us to happiness. Literature has the ability to make us realize that all that goes into making us who we are is worthy of reflection, of remembering.

PrayerStarters

Is there a book that really moves you?

What is it?

Find a particularly poignant passage, and reflect on it.

Dear God,
   I know that your voice speaks to me in so many different ways. Let me hear your voice in this book, and let its words help give me that which I need.

Poetry as Prayer

"The world is so great and rich, and life so full of variety, that you can never lack occasions for poems."
—Goethe, as quoted in *Conversations with Goethe*

Many people say, "I don't read poetry," but wouldn't hesitate to use poetry when they say phrases such as "gentle as a lamb" or "music to my ears." Poetry is not about making things rhyme; it is about expressing just a facet of life in this rich world, filled with variety.

Poetry can help us express facets of our own lives as well. Whereas no one can fully understand our struggles, we can give God and those around us an inkling of what we feel by the use of words—ours or others'—that serve as a portrait of ourselves: complex, colorful, beautiful.

PrayerStarters

How do you feel today?

What images could you come up with that describe that feeling?

Write a poem to God, painting a picture of your life. Know that God will be pleased.

Praying the Song in Your Heart

"Where there's music there can be no evil."
—Cervantes, *Don Quixote*

From the soft lullaby of a mother singing her baby to sleep, to the brash sounds of a Sousa march; from the heart-aching beauty of Mozart's *Requiem*, to the melancholy of the Beatles' *Yesterday*; from the freedom of jazz, to the precision of a drum line: whatever the style, whatever our tastes, music has the ability to lift us out of ourselves into a new realm, to soothe and heal.

PrayerStarters

Pick your favorite piece of music, and listen to it.

Imagine that each note, each beat, has the ability to refresh your soul, to help make you whole.

Dear God,
Thank you for the beauty of music. May its sacred nature help make me ever aware of your presence, surrounding me sweetly like the melody of a beautiful song with words that give meaning and focus to my life.

Art Works

*"You use a glass mirror to see your face: you use
works of art to see your soul."*
—George Bernard Shaw, *Back to Methuselah*

Michaelangelo's paintings in the Sistine Chapel are
considered to be some of the most intricate and glori-
ous works of art the world has ever seen. What is perhaps most striking about the paintings is the over-
whelming passion present in them, Love, hate, sin,
judgment, redemption—all of these things are dis-
played in a way that goes beyond the sense of sight,
and touches the very soul. Art has the ability to let us
feel God in our souls, as well as elevate our souls to
the divine.

PrayerStarters

Go to the library and look at a book of great art throughout history.

What piece touches your soul in a unique way?

What is being said to you through this piece?

Dear God,

I thank you for the beauties of the world of art. In a world where I can be far too preoccupied with the ugly nature of things, help me to see that your beauty is present. May this beauty touch my soul, and reassure me of the beauty of humanity.

Sadness Needs Its Time

*"Into each life some rain must fall,
Some days must be dark and dreary."*
—Longfellow, "The Rainy Day"

We live in a culture of quick fixes, that frequently makes use of the phrase, "Get over it!" Sadness is seen as something against the natural order, as something that, if present in our life, we need to fix right away, get rid of.

But sadness is a part of life. And whereas it is not healthy to wallow in sadness, and allow it to overtake us, it is nevertheless good to acknowledge the sadness, to express how it affects us. Knowing that some days will be dark, and paying attention to that darkness, can help us be more attuned to the presence of light.

PrayerStarters

Make a list of those things that cause you to feel sad.

_____   _____   _____

_____   _____   _____

_____   _____   _____

Dear God,

Help me to know that feeling sad is a part of life. Please be present to me in my sadness, and allow me to learn from its presence in my life without it taking over my life.

Refreshing Waters

"...suddenly he stood by the edge of a full-fed river...All was ashake and ashiver—glints and gleams and sparkles, rustle and swirl, chatter and bubble. The Mole was bewitched, entranced, fascinated."

—Kenneth Grahame, *The Wind in the Willows*

There is something exceedingly captivating about water. The waves of the ocean, a rushing river, a calm lake, a warm bath: all of these images have the ability to capture a different part of our soul, to call to mind varying realities, to bewitch, entrance, and fascinate.

God's love itself can be likened to water. Like a warm bath, it can soothe us; like a cold swim on a spring day, it can refresh us; like the waters of a lake at sunrise, it can be a reminder of true beauty; like a cool washcloth on a feverish head, it can be a relief.

PrayerStarters

Reflect on the image of a river.

What in your life needs to be touched by the life-giving water?

Dear God,
    May your love so wash over me that I can feel my weariness refreshed, my wounds cleansed, and the thirsting in my soul slaked.

Sensing the Seasons

"Sing a song of seasons!
Something bright in all!
Flowers in the Summer,
Fires in the Fall."

—Robert Louis Stevenson, "Autumn Fires"

The senses are most powerful stimulators of memories. The sound of leaves crunching under feet, the smell of apple pie, the feeling of a warm blanket on a cool evening, the sense of season—these things combine within us and help us to see the continuity of life, of God's hand gently guiding the course of nature.

Our lives, too, reflect the seasons. Trusting in God, we can know that the warmth and life of spring will always follow the darkest, coldest winter.

PrayerStarters

Reflect on your favorite season.

What images/sensations come to mind or heart when reflecting?

Dear God,
Help me to know that you are near, as one period of my life turns to another. Help me to thank you for the brightness of summer, the ambiguity of autumn, the darkness of winter, and the sheer promise of the spring.

Everyday Nourishment

"While in their joy they were disbelieving and still wonder-ing, he said to them, "Have you anything here to eat?"
—Luke 24: 41

One thing that is common among all cultures is making a ritual out of eating. Most grand events in life are celebrated with the sharing of a meal. Food can be a portal to the sacred; it can be a common reminder of the unity that exists between human beings, our common bond.

All too often we rush through meals not giving much thought to the act of eating itself. We use the term "fast food" so much now, that it is as if we think that's the way food should be. Eating, sharing a meal, savoring tastes—all of these are gifts from God, and we need to remind ourselves of that from time to time.

PrayerStarters

———— ✦ ————

The next time you gather at table, say a prayer of blessing to God, but slowly, savoring each word, each image in the prayer, as if it were a part of a sumptuous feast in and of itself. Recognize that God is offering this food, this presence to you to strengthen your body and spirit.

Bless us, O Lord,
And these your gifts,
Which we are about to receive from your bounty.

Relaxing in God

"And on the seventh day God finished the work that he had done, and he rested on the seventh day from all the work that he had done."

—Genesis 2: 2

Whether it's ten minutes of shut-eye after reading the paper, or a two-hour-pajamas-on-under-the-covers-Sunday-afternoon slumber, a nap has the ability to refresh us just enough to face the world and its challenges a little more strengthened, a little more renewed.

Too many people think of naps as a waste of time, but these people don't know what they are missing. Just as God rested and reflected on what he had done, so we too should follow that divine example, and immerse ourselves in the sacred, refreshing nature of sleep.

PrayerStarters

Take some time out of this day to rest for a while, sleeping if possible.

Imagine as you rest that God's hand is at work within you, soothing your hurt, strengthening you for life.

Dear God,
As you protect me when I am awake, so watch over me as I sleep. So that when awake I may be mindful of the wonders of your creation, and when asleep rest secure in your peace.

God's Breath, Our Breath

"And when he had said this, he breathed on them and said, 'Receive the Holy Spirit.'"

—John 20: 22

In many ancient languages, the words for "breath" and "spirit" are virtually the same. Ancient peoples easily saw a connection between the breath that allows us to go on and the animating Spirit of God. God's breath, our breath: somehow there is an intimate connection.

Breath itself can become a reminder that God dwells within us. If our breath is labored from illness, God struggles with us. If our breath is rushed with excitement, God shares our stirring. If our breath is weary from sorrow, God laments with us.

PrayerStarters

Find a quiet place to sit.

Breathe slowly in, slowly out, for a few minutes, being aware of your breath.

Imagine that each breath in is filling your body with God's healing love, and that each breath out is expelling that which is harmful and negative.

Dear God,
    Make your breath my breath.

Strolling With Your Soul

"Only those thoughts that come by walking have any value."

—Fredrick Nietzsche, *Twilight of the Idols*

The notion of pilgrimage has long been an important part of the spiritual life. There is something significant in the image of one setting sights on a goal, and, through moving towards that goal, making it a reality, allowing thoughts explored on the journey to bring wisdom and insight.

Whereas few people have the opportunity to make extensive pilgrimages, anyone can benefit from the simple action of walking, or of some other form of movement. It is on the journey, and because of the journey, that God's will for us is laid out. We only need go after it.

PrayerStarters

What is it that you most need from God?

See that need as a destination, a goal.

Go for a walk, and imagine that each step, each movement, is somehow bringing you closer to that destination.

Dear God,
Let me know that not only are you the ultimate destination of every journey, but that your presence itself energizes my steps. Let me feel you walking with me along the way.

Silent Treatment

"Elected Silence, sing to me
And beat upon my whorlèd ear,
Pipe me to pastures still and be
The music that I care to hear."
—Gerard Manley Hopkins, "The Habit of Perfection"

We live in a noisy world. The blare of television sets, the clamor of traffic, the competing voices of people shouting for attention: all of this can combine into such noisy racket that the simplest and sweetest melodies can be overtaken, lost.

There is perhaps no melody sweeter than silence. Silence has the ability to stir our hearts with its simplicity, to quiet our souls to hear God's very song, to feel the presence of music in our lives that, at times, seem far from musical.

PrayerStarters

Find a place—a church, the woods, a room in your home—where you can shut out the noises of the world.

Spend some time in silence, listening for God's voice, God's song.

What do you hear?

Dear God,
Help me to quiet my heart, my soul, my very life, so that I can better listen to your words to me. Make these words as a beautiful melody of comfort and strength.

Sacred Touch

*"When Jesus saw her, he called her over and said,
'Woman, you are set free from your ailment.'
When he laid his hands on her, immediately she
stood up straight and began praising God."*
—Luke 13: 12-13

Many parents, when faced with a child's scrape or cut, say, "Let me kiss it and make it better." Scrapes kissed, tummies and backs rubbed, fevered brows soothed, fears hugged away—children seem to know well the power of touch.

As adults our wounds may be too serious to treat with touch alone, but that doesn't discount its power. The embrace of a lover, the hug of a friend—all of these things help us to know we are not alone, that God, through the hands of others, touches our lives.

PrayerStarters

Ask someone you love—a spouse, a trusted friend—for a hug.

Imagine that the arms you feel around you come from God, who longs to strengthen and support you.

Imagine that your arms are an expression of your love for God as well.

Dear God,
As countless others have felt the healing presence of love through touch, so may the touch that I experience awaken that within me that needs to be whole. May I never doubt your love for me.

"Make Me a Miracle"

"Awe came upon everyone, because many wonders and signs were being done by the apostles."
—Acts of the Apostles: 2:43

Miracles just don't seem to happen as often as they did in days gone by. Maybe the scientific and medical sophistication that humanity has achieved has so become a part of our experience that what was once mistaken for miraculous is now commonplace, a normal part of everyday life.

But miracles can still happen. And whereas it may be foolish to count on a miracle, it is most certainly not foolish to hope for one. Even sophisticated humanity cannot grasp the miraculous wonder of God, in whom all things are possible.

PrayerStarters

Dear God,

Make me mindful of the everyday miracles around me—the perfection of a flower, the brilliance of a sunset, the sheer wonder of the process of life itself. Help me to be thankful for these little miracles, never ignoring their power.

But also, God, if it be your will, make me a miracle as well. Where sickness claims me, bring health; where sorrow wounds my heart, bring joy; where confusion clouds my vision, bring understanding; where anxiety infects me, bring peace.

Believing in God's Love

"Faith is to believe what you do not yet see; the reward for this faith is to see what you believe."
—Saint Augustine

Faith is a vital element of life. It is faith that allows us to move forward in this confusing world, even when there are times that we would rather retreat. It is faith that allows us to forgive when we have been hurt, even when there are times when we would rather stay angry. It is faith that allows us to offer love, even when there are times when we would rather give indifference.

As much as we grow in our belief of those things which we cannot see, there is always more to see. Though at times it may be difficult to even muster a word of prayer, let us never cease praying for faith.

PrayerStarters

Reflect on a loved one whose love for you is beyond doubt.

How do you know that this person loves you?

How has this person shown this love?

Now reflect on God's love for you.

How do you know that God loves you?

How has God shown this love?

Dear God,
    Increase my faith, so that I may know you better.

Wanting What God Wants

"Father, for you all things are possible; remove this cup from me; yet, not what I want, but what you want."

—Mark 14: 36

There is a huge difference between resignation to God's will and giving up. When we give up, we, in essence, are saying that the fight was not worth it, the battle a waste of our time. When we resign ourselves to God's will, we are saying that, even if we don't care too much for the outcome, there was something to be said for doing what we could.

We are not always going to like what life has to offer us, and we can fight it. But in the end, in the midst of the mystery of God's plan, we ultimately have to pray that our wills become somehow conformed to the will of God.

PrayerStarters

Dear God,

    I am feeling burdened in my life right now because of _____.
If possible, I would like for you to free me from these burdens. But if that is not your plan, then I would ask that you help me to accept your plan, to learn what you have to teach me.

About the Author

   Father Alaric Lewis, O.S.B., is a Benedictine monk and priest of Saint Meinrad Archabbey in southern Indiana, where he serves as the abbey's Choirmaster. He dedicates this book to his family and the parishioners of St. Anthony of Padua Parish in Effingham, Illinois, whose love and prayers were instruments of God's healing for him.

PrayerStarters Series

--- ✍ ---

- *PrayerStarters in Times of Pain or Illness*
  by Alaric Lewis, O.S.B. #20110

- *PrayerStarters to Help You Handle Stress*
  by Molly Wigand #20107

- *PrayerStarters for Busy People*
  by Daniel Grippo #20109

- *PrayerStarters to Help You Heal After Loss*
  by Elizabeth Stalling #20108

Available at your favorite bookstore or gift shop, or
directly from: One Caring Place, Abbey Press,
St. Meinrad, IN 47577
(800) 325-2511